FI

Philomena Ewing

PALORES PUBLICATIONS' 21st CENTURY WRITERS

Philomena Ewing
Floating in the Blue

August 2007

ISBN 978-0-9556682-0-3

Published by:

Palores Publications,
11a Penryn Street,
Redruth,
Cornwall.
TR15 2SP

Designed and printed by:

ImageSet,
63 Tehidy Road,
Camborne,
Cornwall.
TR14 8LJ
01209 712864

Typeset in Garamond 10/11pt

For Colin (Santiago),
who is the love and joy of my life,
with all my love and thanks.
You sustain me
ad infinitum.

We shall not cease from exploration
and the end of all our exploring
will be to arrive where we started
and know the place for the first time.

T.S. Eliot

All paths lead to the same goal,
to convey to others what we are.

Pablo Veruda

LIST OF CONTENTS

On Foreign Ground

On foreign ground,
where all the attention is given to the sets
and the costumes,
the hidden crocodile
lying low
in the shadow of
the sheltering sky,
remembered
moving pictures.

Luckily it came out on a hot Saturday afternoon
in midsummer, so nobody saw it.

Across the forehead, the viewer's gaze is directed
across the line of the eyes;
the details of skin and features,
the apparently impassive expression.

There was no hint of aggression,
no self-conscious search for style.
The eyes reflect myself in him and him in me.

I can see a winning breakfast cereal smile;
savage, sharp-eyed,
the stance is poised,
ready, for the moment of acceleration.

Communion.
He oversees the sticks, stones and broken bones.
He's eating his way to a heart condition

Face the tree which the earth settlers had recently uprooted
with earth-moving equipment.
The roots are hanging out sideways,
tanglings lost
in the chalky earth pulled up with them.
Such a tree is more than 150 years old.
They brought houses with wheels and big ploughs
and night and day they were ripping up the land.
The army came down at night with power saws.

Are the two conquests really so very different ?
Please respond,
All seeing, all knowing and the Word made flesh.

Internet Culture

You're my hyperlink Baby.
You're the icon of my screen.
You've such an appealing interface.
You're the applet of my dreams.

You were dragged and dropped
from a one stop shop
on life's information superhighway,
but now you're compressed on my hard disk space
in gigabyte domains.

I was interrupted by your kiss
from an ethereal http address;
now I'm pixelated and resonating
in waves of data streams.

At first I thought your file transfer protocol
left a lot to be desired,
encrypted as it was in some acrobatic dot;
a macroviral bullet in disguise

But soon I was upgraded
to your cute little modem ways
and quickly learnt to navigate
round your worldwide cyberspace.

And when your browser adjusted
to suddenly download on me,
the shockwave of on-line jamming
brought me to html ecstasy.

And sometime in the third millennium
down that old Feng Shui way,
we'll scroll bar through our floppy discs
down microsoft's sweet memory lane,

To remember how late one Valentine's Eve,
back in nineteen ninety eight,
two half hearted clicks on some j. peg. gifs,
fused our anima and animus together.

Murphy's Poem

Isn't it strange, thought Murphy,
now that I'm dead,
how green the trees are looking
in their Sunday best,
and isn't it grand that I have flowers
lying over my head
and the people saying prayers,
for my soul's eternal rest.

Isn't it strange, thought Paddy,
now that Murphy's dead,
that the colours of the world
seem so grey and drab;
and isn't it sad that the wreath
I sent him is dead,
and the God that I believed in
is no longer in my head.

Isn't it strange, thought God,
now that Murphy's dead,
that heaven is full of laughter
and earth should be so sad;
and isn't it me that is the creator
of all that's good and bad,
and the people I created
I no longer wish I had.

Which Way is Out?
(A lupper is polari for a hand)

Was the queen
coming in?
or was she
storming out?
For when
her picture
it was taken,
there seemed to be
some doubt.
Was her crown
giving her gip?
Did she bite
her bottom lip,
fearing she
was going
to trip?
or was she
simply happy
to be
having
a lovely day,
doing
all the things
that queenies do,
in that
regal
sort of way?

There's nothing like
being a queen,
for it's often
so nice to be seen,
by all those
loyal subjects
jostling to shake ones lupper,
but sometimes
when it gets dull,
and one thinks
it's a load of bull,
then it's best
to head for home
and get a
Tesco Home Delivery in
for supper.

Was the queen
coming in?
or was she
going out?
for the photographs
that were taken
had confused
the entire nation,
causing
much exasperation
in the
British Broadcasting Corporation.

So here's
the explanation,
so there'll be
no consternation.
They were simply back to front:
and the one of her storming out
was just one of her rushing in,
and so the moral
of this tale,
so that
harmony should prevail,
is that
one should
never fail
to check
your photos
are arranged
in
the correct direction.

Terrorist Cells

Between 9.30 and 9.45 a.m. on a Sunday at mass,
I shut my eyes tightly to pray hard.
I tried to remove distractions of all that was around:
the red sacred heart and the candles aglow.
The quality of silence was good, with
practised contemplation and meditation;
so good I was almost comatose,
but the echoes of war blasted out:
I can't remember peace in me.
I can't remember peace in me.

Between 10.30 and 11 a.m. on a Sunday after mass,
I read the papers of Glasgow airport suicide bombers.
I saw burnt flesh and red blood
and later found that two doctors were involved.
Baffled, sad and angry, I could not see how to forgive.
Everything went round and round in my head:
I can't remember peace in me.
I can't remember peace in me.

Between 12 o'clock and 4 a.m. on Monday
I had chilling dreams of ram raids and fire bombs.
I heard controlled explosions
ripping through the flesh of my neighbours,
memories of suspicious behaviour
in the heart of the rush hour
dogs sniffing and police swooping:
I can't remember peace in me.
I can't remember peace in me.

I woke up Monday in a bad mood
and I was caught up with washing and tidying.
I was hurrying around and the wind was so strong
the garage door was blown off its hinges
and my world was turned upside down:
I can't remember peace in me.
I can't remember peace in me

All day, every day, armed police were hunting down terrorists,
flights were axed and passengers unpacked suspect packages,
to find incendiary devices among suntan lotions and babies milk
and everyone was frisked whilst the waiting line stretched
on and on, and no one could resist the latest video game
of trying to compile the profile of a terrorist.
Softly spoken; nice guy; very friendly; good student; family man.

Allegedly this and allegedly that filled the air.
Sources say... .
I can't remember peace in me.
I can't remember peace in me.

Out on the road South of Kandahar, the opium poppies grow;
their scarlet red hearts release millions of seeds of terror cells
and receive an offer of alliance from the windy desert air.
Swirling from the interior ministry of sound,
their call to all crusaders echoes down the years:

All I ever wanted was to remember peace in me.
All I ever wanted... .... was peace in me.

The paradox
of our acts.

Twelve Eejits

Twelve eejits standing grinning,
be-grudging gombeens,
spinning gobbets of discontent,
stalking talkers slobbering.

Twelve eejits standing skulking,
blinking frame-ups,
serrated smiles behind hooded eyes,
supercilious stonkings of scum.

Twelve eejits standing innocently,
bubbling their hideous assertions,
stigmatising seismic ostracisms,
subterranean plotters snuffing me out.

Twelve eejits standing willingly,
belching bagatelles of poison,
sealskin tight with pallid expressions,
small heads their swollen shadows spreading.

Twelve eejits standing smiling,
back sliding butter upperers,
succulent traitors fecund with rumours,
stomachs and viscera full of lying

Twelve eejits standing quietly,
bluffing butchers blunting fidelity,
surgically suffocating the truth,
stealing my life away silently.

Twelve eejits, I've news for you.
Behind me now you all stand.
Such are my scars of integrity,
safely they're healing in history.

PATER NOSTER

Our Father	Eternal Ovipositor
Who art in heaven	Immortal genome
Hallowed be thy name	H.U.G.O Watson and Crick
Thy kingdom come	Monsanto, Zeneca and Novartis
Thy will be done	Multiple drug resistance
On earth as it is in heaven	Living wills
Give us this day	Hospice skills
Our daily bread	Morphine pills and clones
And forgive us our trespasses	Genetic drift and antigenic shift
As we forgive those	Ecological terrorists
Who trespass against us	MRSA
And lead us not into temptation	Euthanasia
But deliver us from Evil	Mercy killing ~ You decide
Amen	So be it

Night Fever (or F in this ..... F   in that or just F words).

The hot sweat
that trailed down her back
and chest, at fifty years of age
was menopausal;
at least she figured that was the cause,

But the figure hugging heat gave no respite,
from ten o'clock at night
until six the next morning for several weeks,
bringing more obsessive fears
that it was something much more serious
than fiery hormonal swings.
She dreamed on in a frumpish heap.

She fantasised that the heat was from feral cells
in her lungs fermenting.
Beneath her feigned indifference
lay a foreboding of
full blown cancer.

The cause perhaps, lay in
foolhardy life -choices she had made;
full fat foods,
full bodied wines,
forbidden fruits.

All the fury inside was
from festered life,
fractional failures,
foul ups
and fusillades of abuse, laid down
in her fast track life,
from lack of fortitude.

All the futile attempts
to take the right fork in the road
at the right time,
were forerunners of her fate,
inside this cellular hotbed fusion reactor.

She lay in bed hoping that the febrile heat was benign,
nothing more than a faltering hypothalamus;
a fatigued pituitary gland
readjusting to the decline of oestrogen.
She knew that it was a fire alarm;

that her shelf life was
coming to an end,
so she had to show fortitude.

She took classes in neuro linguistic programming
in the forlorn hope that
she could re-figure and reframe it.
She lay around feeling feckless and frumpish .
Every night she remained fettered
to the fireball within.

Then her mind ran to Hephaestus
and using fuzzy logic
she made a decision that this fruitless body
was now instead a full time refinery,
and that her remaining task although finicky,
would be to re - fashion these bodily changes into fine filigree.

She would subvert this raging fever
 into a fuel injection.
She would use it as high octane fuel.
She would funnel it
 into a life changing renewal programme;
a focused poultice in a fourth dimension.

She re-took classes in neuro linguistic programming
and now found them fun,
and although she faltered from time to time,
she eventually found herself in fine fettle.

She fumigated the house.
She bought a new front door,
and refurbished the house.
For the first time in a long time
she found she was able
to look at herself in the mirror
in full frontal view,
in fully fashioned stockings.

She became a fundraiser for charities,
did fun runs,
went to funfairs.
She played funky music.
She was now a foxy lady,
fulfilled,
fully fledged,
forgiven,
In the fullness of her own time.

Lives in St Ives

In St Ives the scalloped edges
of peoples lives
are picked at by seagulls and scavengers.
Dive bombing in, they cause such a din
and leave their detritus behind

In St Ives the rufflled feathers
of peoples lives
are nipped at by seagulls and strangers.
Fiddling on in, they are as sharp as a pin
and as cruel as the changes in weather

In St Ives the rough seas
of peoples lives
are stormed at by seagulls and sailors.
Swinging on down, they are run aground
and hung out to dry by tomorrow.

In St Ives the sunlit faces
of peoples lives
are focused on by seagulls and painters.
Sweeping on in, they are copied and framed
and sold at exorbitant prices.

ART AS SIMPLE AS ABC

Artists, artisans, artefacts.
Work is defined by ABC 's,
but so ill at ease
inside categories
for abstract, traditional and craft.

It sounded simple,
but could not be done,
for in every nook and cranny,
the whispering dark forces
threatened to consume them.

Enthralled by florid language,
Narcissus was moonstruck
and pretended to shed a tear.
Do not be fooled,
it was just an ideogram,
a maladroit performance.

The true night fishermen
would never pang
or desire with guile, to separate
and then pretend to reparate.
In apparition they showed contempt.

Neoteny spread
like quicksilver
in the shallow brush marks
that left skewered images of ordinariness
bound by irrevocable malcontent.

Alluding,
always alluding,
in glitzy reflection,
but never in humility
or by consensus.
Their power was lost
in battlefields past,
lost in the rituals of war
and aggravations,
the first bombardment of liberty.

The liminal zone they sought,
the magic eye,
could never be acquired
in spreading brush
or ochre

Self ground paints,
or machine made hues,
it made no difference to the view.
It was still hyped obsessions,
grotesque impressions.

They dredged them to the surface
but they became
reflective surfaces,
to be walked upon.

In every gliding stroke
ingressed infidelities were
caught in the crosswinds of guilt;
the art a mere marriage of convenience
gone to ground.

The maelstroms glide path
passed to the next generation,
virulent structural formulas,
imperceptible collisions,
like father, like son.

Clearing the space,
The tide moves in.
The smooth bright waves stain the sand
to patchy grains
of remembrance.

Lie there, infixed,
sticking to the watermark,
gripping the high edge of the world,
that holds up to the light
and elements,

the moment before the ebbing current
sucks you slowly back,
till you are dripping
and foaming
for lack of faith.

Know that the sea has no need for emblems,
nor landscapes need for modernity or modernism.
The sea is just the sea, startling
The earth, the rocks, the salt.
Believe.

Expansive and supple,
equal to everything you could ever give
or take from it.
So much more yielding
in its burden heaving.

It's past grown and groaning,
with beauty and atrocity,
equally sophisticated in verse or fiction,
making all sense and nonsense,
muffling all human sounds.

Its inherent senses say
Adore,
Obey.
You say too much.
Drown in me.

The Muses

All the love of the muses
have flowered in a lonely word.
All the hopes and verdant wishes
have been watered in the soil of life;
all rooted in the nurseries of the soul.
Know this nature well,
for it will never betray
the heart that grows to love me.

The Medusa stare of the female through tangled hair,
the hunky body of the male on the stair,
whatever floats your boat, or turns you on
mentally,
physically,
spiritually,
let them in imagining;
let yourself out to meet them.

Ride with them through your own country.
Show them the wilderness that you came from.
Run through the open ground,
charged with your history and beginnings.
Sleep with them on cliff top;
in burnished images of all the films
and filmstars you would like to be,
all rolled into one giant subpersonality;

Jane Fonda before she got bossy,
the left profile of Dirk Bogarde,
Audrey Hepburn outside Tiffany's before breakfast,
Lauren Bacall at any age;
Blondie before she got old,
Gregory Peck in to Kill a Mockingbird,
Annie Lennox in full flow,
Chrissie Hynd not pretending;
Paul Newman and Daniel Craig in anything.

Via positiva Via negativa

Upright primate
whatever you believe in,
take some time
to leave the confines of yourself.
Accept the invitation
to look up
through the skies,
up to the deepest view you have ever had
of this dense dark blanket of space.

Know the vista is not your invention.

Then cast your eyes to the ground below
and look carefully
at the myriad world teeming within,
where in one gram of soil
ten thousand million species grow.

Know now you are not the sole owner
of this floor to ceiling canvas.

Where the land slopes to the sea,
wind, water, light and darkness toil.
Not on your behalf does this spectacle unfold.
You can be ignored.

The dark alchemy of transformation
may allow you to see that
all you do these days is
cut and paste
from the scrapyards of your waste.

You don't know what goes on inside the box
fall /redemption,
body/soul,
matter/spirit,
natural/supernatural:
you have no idea at all.

Know what you are
and look beyond your boastful self
to see and understand
the journey and its goal are intermingled.

Know that each one of the specks in your eye
twelve billion
light years away,
is a galaxy of stars and planets,
feeble and incoherent reflections entwined.

Know that each one of the specks in your eye
contains a thousand billion universes
to which wandering magi
you do not even know of
will travel to,
bearing gifts
to something their minds cannot grasp,
but which they recognise
as so much more sublime and
greater than themselves.

The future is out there.
Let go.
Be nurtured.
Be transformed.

Seasonal Affective Disorder or S.A.D.

Today reminded her of seasons.
Spring full of hope and reason,
roots solidly folded into burgeoning wet soil,
childhood dreams with no sense of toil,
lightly playing gold leaves, unfurling virgin foil.

Today, the summer optimism is thriving.
She sets off to go to school, but really she was skiving.
She runs off to the woods and playing fields and tennis greens,
bronzed and skipping in full cry, the hullabaloo of dreams.

Today the Autumn breaks the spell and stealth returns.
The biting winds, grey mists and darkness of early night spurns.
Her smiles droop and she begins to frown.
She feels herself beginning to drown
out the clamour of blue oceans and unfurled skies.
In melatonin surplus memory, dreamily she lies.

Today winter bites and cuts into her face.
She has lost the quickening elastic pace
and her frosty expression resolutely stores up work for miles.
She cannot seem to shirk the wrinkled work set in piles.
Her duties are always en suite.
This year's beat is nearly complete, but strangely it is still only July.

What has happened to this solo rhythm of life she travelled?
Her personal trauma has become unravelled,
and is now a global distress.
The world is a mess
She can only guess staying alive
is the only option left... ., for all of us.

Doppelganger

Do not be afraid to look at me.
Because of you, I am in reach of the rain,
or in the sunlight, I am a prism,
dancing in chaos and complexity.

By the wayside you are there.
In the darkness of the tunnel,
in the brightness of your glare,
you guide me around the corner,
through the window prised open,
your mixed blessings make their home.
Between repeated lines
of failure and success,
dizzily, you blind me.

Do not be afraid to touch me.
If not for your feathered touch,
there could never be the search
for daring love poems,
shifting sands,
sure foundations,
all becoming serendipity,
from total wastes of time.

Do not be afraid to listen to me.
Because of you my uvula vibrates,
through empty space,
on to hammer, anvil and stirrup,
then to inner ear,
where snail like extractions
amplify and make mature,
your signature tessitura,
your personal stamp of approval to my utterings.

Do not be afraid to look at me.
For you are my perfect fit,
my healing spirit,
on the curving wave
of emerald time,
just before breaking,
close up;
liberating
my dark lonely heart with your beauty.

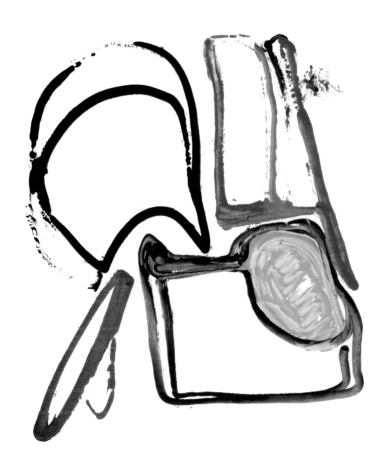

Boost

I'm not into boosting your ego.
That's not what I'm about.
For like inflated balloons,
sooner or later they pop.
I'm not into using or abusing.
That's not what I'm about.
For like people treated as objects,
sooner or later they're dropped.
I'm not into much of a muchness.
That's not what I'm about.
I'm into trying and failing,
and making crooked lines straight.
I'm into tender embraces,
tears that can turn into joy.
I'm into trying to make selfishness we-ness.
I'm hoping that I will grow small.
I'm into the art of loving;
Truth is I know .... all !

Don't Fence Me In

Don't fence me in,
or I will rage,
like a hammer headed bull,
to drive a nail through your bleeding heart.

Pasture me in open fields,
and I will graze contented at your feet.
For there is power and *Power*,
One is to love, the other to hate.

One enslaves,
One liberates.

Don't fence me in,
or I will stir the blackness sleeping
into blazing day,
to burn you in a fire,
aglow with broken promises.

Long Distance

Let us trade defiance

We have trawled

tonight

to soul and back

rapier sharp

verbal virtuosity

laughter in your eyes

When you snatch away

for openness

through everything

 from trivia

your words were

dazzlingly swift

displayed with such wit

sparkling and alive

the connection

Then you cut the conversation

Or you stop "tuning in"

 when you keep me on

that for me is hell

when you are "bored"

 your boredom serves you well

"long distance"

Holding Ourselves Together

For the conversations that are being refused;
for the realm of the unspoken;
for the way we stupidly
spend so much time and effort,
holding ourselves together,
by keeping things apart.

For the questions that have no replies;
for the barbed wire imprints on our lives;
for the blank spaces filled with backward looks
stained bleeding on the ground;
hopelessly poor choices leap and tear at us
but giddily we stumble forward.

For the trembling moments of truth;
for the shy intimacy of flesh;
for the sieving of timidity
straining messages of solidity;
hungrily we are strung together
by this strange canopy of love.

Colours We Wear

Domes of ignorance block our way.
Words are not helpful for the things we need to say,
but beneath the blunders, everything still gets said,
in the colours we wear
or when our eyes meet in bed.
I am not uncomfortable
in long silences, as long as
they are nothing to do with evasion.
I can find my way through the cracks;
All I need is your persuasion.
Towers of reticence can soon be dismantled;
It all depends on how they are handled.

Throwing a Wobbly

Throwing a wobbly
now and again,
seems in order,
just to work things out;
someone has to fall;
and sometimes in falling,
we land together,
better for the fall.
Landing on a bed of nails
can be a piercing experience.
When trouble is part of our lives
if we don't share it sometimes,
then we don't give
the person who loves us,
a chance to love us, enough.

In Time

You can be ferocious
brusque and abrupt,
boiling over sometimes
in love.

You can be raging
frantic and strong,
discharging anger, sometimes
in love.

You can storm me,
convulse me,
thunder and explode
but always, always
quenched
in love.

As if you have things to say
that never might be said
in time.

Subdued Light

Like myself, these pictures
look better in subdued light,
where shadows gently linger,
as the day slips into night;
where the deepest thoughts
and longings stir,
beneath all others sight;
where you think
there are only ashes,
and you think the fire is out,
what can stir a human heart?
what can remove all doubt?
Only love given freely,
then the flame burns bright,
and the darkest days of winter
are embers burning white,
in the sparkle of your love,
you give me love of life.

leafy love

stories to be written,
homage to be paid,
submerged memories,
shrouded in layers
upon the page are laid;
sanctified and sanitised,
hallowed be their names,
hollowed out to some degree
in the shadow and the shade;
the life and touch and taste of me
only in your arms are contained;
and if there are words
that can convey the love I feel for you,
let them ring out loudly
from every tree top crown
and every slender leaf,
blown down wind down.

EGG

No egg for breakfast?
No, I didn't mean
what I said.
I really did want one
but I pretended
I didn't , instead.
Sausages and mushrooms-
bacon and toasted bread
I said, were fine.
But I knew, so when I got home
I drew you an egg.
As Roger Hilton said
"It's not what you put in that is important
It's what you leave out."

Shells

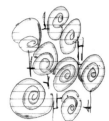

When we hurt one another
we sometimes retreat;
inside our respective shells,
to heal or to sleep;
deep within,
to shut out the world,
its clamour and its din.
When tired and depleted,
dried up in speech and thought,
we need to listen in the silence... .
felt absence, felt love.
Always, when we are like this,
we come together again.
Slowly your strength and your power move over me
and I give myself to you;
deep inside me, perfectly formed,
complete in your love for me.

Amygdala and Almonds

Feel the robust memory,
the milk of almonds,
foreseeable
in that special time and place,
and then the emotion
that follows
and overtakes thoughts, deeds and words.
Find what bitter antiques lie here,
sugar coated ambassadors,
watching over words
to perform them,
or leave them
shelled out,
burnt blossoms;
activists
ready to drop;
backlogged,
stockpiled,
pasted,
as forensic accountants.

Flaked,
forsaken,
green, opaque;
disturbed and revoked,
straining me to the limit.
Ticking timebombs
suspended;
yet can also be
up and running in no time.
In some cases found wanting,
in others a watchful promise
of things yet to come.

Veterans,
Casualties,
Survivors,
Relics.

Floating in the Blue

Some people are pale
and tight - lipped;
cautious, cold and calculating.
But in your eyes
there is relaxed warmth and longing
and I feel us both stretching out,
in a deep blue pool,
where we both lie laughing
and we keep on loving
and your eyes water,
lapped by the rolling waves,
floating in the blue.

Back from Milan,
we missed the Italian dream.
Two years later,
Three years later,
we are no longer old.
We are better than ever,
in a certainty of place,
in the heart of time,
in a deep blue pool,
where we both lie laughing,
and we keep on loving,
floating in the blue.

Autobiography of a Cloud Maker
(somewhere on the West coast of Cornwall).

Clearly, today for Western dwellers my changing state will irritate for they would like a better blue with reddish hue to close their evening in their extended garden rooms. Daring to experiment would take some time in this frenetic world of climate change and I am tempted to revert to more classic varieties of cloud formation even though it will not get the same attention. Monogrammed clouds used to be my cosy signature piece; well thought of by day dreamers, Laurence Llewellyn-Bowen types or urban downsizers to country-cottage lifestyles. But lately all my work seems so last year, dull and boring.

Down, up and round - framing the idea of a new cloud design without compromising on style was always so easy for me. Sea grass chill, Rapunzel like plumes, chip shop curry colours and flocculating agents added to give the final texture. I would fling them like woven scatter cushions across the punctured sky. Eclectic mixes of mirrored sheets were so eye catching to anyone driving home from work who cared to look up. There were many days when I was young and learning the craft when I was liberated from the need to be functional and learnt more experimental techniques. Those were the heady days when an ancient craft slowly developed into a serious art form.

I learnt the technical stuff quickly. Cloud Studies and Global Climate Risk Assessment seminars came much later in my career. Last month I went to Greenland and learnt to specialise in darker blues and warmer terracotta hues over the ice floes. Cloud making is a hands-on craft. The old timers are still enthusiastic about the old varieties of cloud like Pig Snout so well suited to local conditions but traditional layouts no longer seem to work. You have to go with the flow. Weather making must be seen as an organic entity, forever evolving.

The demands made on today's weather makers are very different from those of a generation ago. Cloud makers these days are never still. We drift in and out with unexplainable moods and feelings through milky white light. My work is inspired by memories and half-forgotten moments in time. As a sculptor, I work with small scale maquettes and move on to larger pieces. I enjoy the larger freer pieces with shorter life spans that can be exhibited in wide open spaces. Large scale installation pieces take several months to prepare. Even when I make scale models it is difficult to imagine how it will look in the space of the open sky. I worry about so many things; the size and whether the clouds will look finished enough in the context of the seasons. Plagiarism is a problem. Raising basic standards is a problem. We can no longer have only 20% of student cloud makers reaching the highest grades. Free flowing open plan layouts and careful clutter control are all ways of achieving the new skies so popular today.

A lot of us have been suffering from seasonal affective disorder since the clocks went back and we long for a blast of brilliance - something exuberant - perhaps a showcase installation would be allowed for a few hours.

In these winter days when we are all on full-time cloud cover, vital decisions have to be made about colour, shape, texture and surfaces. I desperately need something with a soft sheen to take away my sombre palette.

Space management is critical and we always argue over the meagre times we are given to de-clutter. Cloud appreciation is shifting. We need to demonstrate the possibilities of combining art with the excellence of craftsmanship.

I often chat with my fellow cloud makers about the link between the technical and the creative process. "Cloudscapes" - timeless looks for coastal living that blend with the natural environment. Contemporary styling with a country feel - that timeless craftsmanship is still needed but minimalist is in now. The contemporary on - the - edge wild cloud makers are the inspiration for us all now. Each cloud requires up to ten separate moulds and when the cloud is ready to be removed from its cast the pieces are remoulded on an impressive scale before more experimental sculpturing techniques are used to give the final product. The world of cloud making is now a minefield of technicalities, but as the human race has usurped our art I am saddened at the loss of all I could once do.

Rain, then showers, moderate becoming good
Cyclonic, becoming East or North East
Storm Ten at first
Wintry showers, moderate or poor
Rising slowly, falling slowly
Wind South, South East.
Slight drizzle
A depression
Rain later
Showers, then rain
Steady
One thousand and one
Now falling